Edward

The last installment of your
favorite series —

Mom + Dad.

Roald Dahl's EVEN MORE REVOLTING RECIPES

Introduced by Felicity Dahl • Illustrated by Quentin Blake
Photographs by Jan Baldwin • Recipes by Lori-Ann Newman

VIKING

To Roald's grandchildren and to my grandchildren — F.D.

Sophie

Clover

Luke

Phoebe

Chloe

Billy

Ned

Edie

Oscar

Max

Samuel

COOK'S NOTES

**These recipes are for the family to enjoy making together.
Some could be dangerous without the help of an adult.
Children, please have an adult with you when you are using
knives, handling anything hot, or using a food processor.**

VIKING
Published by the Penguin Group, Penguin Putnam Books for Young Readers,
345 Hudson Street, New York, New York 10014, U.S.A.
Penguin Books Ltd, Registered Offices: Harmondsworth, Middlesex, England
First published in the United Kingdom by Jonathan Cape, the Random House Group Limited, 2001
First published in the United States of America by Viking, a division of Penguin Putnam Books for Young Readers, 2001
1 3 5 7 9 10 8 6 4 2
Text copyright © Felicity Dahl and Roald Dahl Nominee Ltd, 2001 • Illustrations copyright © Quentin Blake, 2001
Photographs copyright © Jan Baldwin, 2001 • All rights reserved
Grateful acknowledgment is made for permission to reprint excerpts from the following works:
Charlie and the Chocolate Factory, copyright © 1964 by Roald Dahl; *Danny the Champion of the World*, copyright © 1975 by Roald Dahl;
Fantastic Mr. Fox, copyright © 1970 by Roald Dahl; *James and the Giant Peach*, copyright © 1961 by Roald Dahl. Reprinted by
permission of Alfred A. Knopf Children's Books, a division of Random House, Inc.
The BFG, copyright © 1982 by Roald Dahl; *Boy*, copyright © 1984 by Roald Dahl; *The Giraffe and the Pelly and Me*, copyright © 1985
by Roald Dahl. Reprinted by permission of Farrar, Straus and Giroux, LLC.
Library of Congress Catalog Card Number: 2001135024
ISBN 0-670-03515-7
Printed in Singapore
Royalties from this book will be donated to the Roald Dahl Foundation,
whose aims are to help in the areas of neurology, hematology, and literacy.

Introduction

"Nose bags on!" or **"Grub's up!"** was Roald's way of announcing that the next meal was ready. He would preside at the head of the table in a very large armchair with Chopper, his dog, sitting on the arm beside him eagerly awaiting the ration of Smarties candy that he would be given at the end of the meal.

Roald's fascination with food certainly started at a young age. I remember him describing the start of his holidays at his grandparents' house in Oslo. His maiden aunts would be sitting on the veranda with large bowls of *multer*, a very special yellow blackberry native to Norway. Each of his aunts would be holding a needle, and very carefully, they would examine each berry to see if a little worm was inside, and yes, with the needle they would make a stab and remove it. Roald said that the worms were not stupid. They were always in the sweetest and tastiest of berries.

His mother kept every letter he ever wrote to her from boarding school, neatly tied in small bundles with pink ribbon like barrister's briefs. In these letters he was constantly asking her to send him food — food that was not always easy to post. Can you imagine asking your mother to send you raw eggs?

Thanks awfully, for your letter, and the eggs and the foot stuff. One egg was broken, so we had to throw it away but all the rest were fine. I had two of them poached last night for supper. And that foot powder is jolly good, I put some in this morning.

I hope not *in* the poached eggs!

He also asked her to send him a Primus stove to cook these raw ingredients on. Why? Well, I think the following extract will tell you:

"You see we are'nt allowed to cook supper on the fire on weekdays. But Michael and I had put a small tin of Peasoup in front of the fire to heat — one hour before

supper, which was quite within the law. When I came to take it off, the tin was bulging at both ends, hellish pressure inside owing to the steam of the boiling soup. I covered it with an umbrella and pierced it from behind—then took away the umbrella and stood at a safe distance; an enormous jet of steam and pea soup shot out, and continued to shoot for about 2 minutes—all over the study, the place was covered with condensing pea-soup."

As I continued to read these letters, did I find the seeds of ideas that he later developed in his stories? Here is another extract. What do you think?

Yesterday we had a lecture on China, it was jolly good, and the person described a Chinese Doctor, and said their prescriptions for flu was generally as follows:

A Rats tail
A snake
Chickens legs
Grass
Ashes of paper
Tiger bone-tea
And the shavings of Rhinoceros Horn

Surely, this was the original draft of the centipede's song in *James and the Giant Peach*?

I hope that the recipes in this book will inspire you to be as inventive with your cooking as Roald was with his. I certainly hope that they will not make you suffer from indigestion as he did on January 25, 1930, when he wrote to his mother:

Thanks awfully for the Tablets. I took some a few times and the indigestion has stopped now, they are jolly good.

Felicity Dahl, Gipsy House 2001

Contents

The Royal Breakfast
for growing giants

During the next twenty minutes, a whole relay of footmen were kept busy hurrying to and from the kitchen carrying third helpings and fourth helpings and fifth helpings of fried eggs and sausages for the ravenous and delighted BFG.

—from THE BFG

You will need:

small frying pan
large appetite

1¼ tsp. oil
3 cocktail sausages
3 baby mushrooms
1 piece of bacon cut into small strips
1 cherry tomato
3 quail eggs or 1 chicken egg scrambled
1 slice of bread
butter

1. Heat frying pan on medium setting.

2. Add 1¼ tsp. oil to warm pan.

3. Put sausages and mushrooms into pan and brown all over.

4. Add bacon to pan and cook 2-3 minutes.

5. Slice cherry tomato in half and add—cut side down—to pan. Cook for 2 minutes and carefully turn over.

6. Crack quail eggs into pan and fry until just cooked, with yolk still soft (about 3 minutes). If using chicken egg, crack into a bowl and scramble with a fork. Pour into pan and cook until no longer runny.

7. While egg is cooking, toast bread, butter it, and slice into 3 pieces.

8. Carefully slide everything onto a plate and eat immediately.

Hot-house Eggs

*Nothing could be simpler or sillier than this recipe, but
for some mysterious reason children love it. We always called it*
Hot-house Eggs, *don't ask me why.*
—from ROALD DAHL'S COOKBOOK

Use any type of egg for this recipe. If you are using an ostrich egg, the hole will need to be much bigger, but if you have a nematode egg, which is only .008 inch, you will only need to make a pinprick in the bread.

You will need:

2½″ cookie cutter
frying pan

1 thick slice of bread
½ tbs. oil
1¼ tbs. butter
1 egg

1. Stamp out a hole in the bread with the cookie cutter.

2. Heat frying pan.

3. Add half the oil and butter to the pan.

4. When it starts to bubble, add bread and cutout bit to pan.

5. Fry until golden brown and then flip over.

6. Carefully crack the egg into the hole and fry until the white solidifies. If you like your eggs well done, you can flip the whole thing over and cook on the other side for about 30 seconds with the remaining butter and oil.

7. Serve with cutout bit.

The Hotel Breakfast

Breakfast was the best meal of the day in our hotel, and it was all laid out on a huge table in the middle of the dining-room from which you helped yourself. There were maybe fifty different dishes to choose from on that table.

—from BOY

A slightly simpler version to make at home . . .

SERVES 2

You will need:

11″ nonstick frying pan with ovenproof handle, or an ovenproof dish

6 slices of bacon

5 eggs

salt and pepper

2½ tbs. milk

1. Heat the oven to 400°F.

2. Fry bacon until it starts to get crispy.

3. Crack eggs into a bowl. Mix them with salt, pepper, and milk.

4. Add egg mixture to frying pan. (If you are using an ovenproof dish, place all ingredients in the dish and put it in the oven for 20-25 minutes. Skip to step 8.)

5. Don't stir.

6. Leave on the burner for 1 minute.

7. Put in the oven until the whole thing is puffed up and golden on top (about 15 minutes).

8. Turn out onto a plate and eat.

Hornets Stewed in Tar

"I've eaten fresh mudburgers by the greatest cooks there are,
And scrambled dregs and stinkbugs' eggs and
hornets stewed in tar."
—from JAMES AND THE GIANT PEACH

You will need:

cookie sheet

9″ x 13″ pan

saucepan

one adult

1¾ c. mixed seeds—
  pumpkin seeds,
  sunflower seeds,
  sesame seeds, pine
  nuts, and poppy
  seeds (keep poppy
  seeds separate from
  the other seeds)

2½ c. sugar

1¾ c. water

juice of ½ lemon
  (1 tbs.)

1¼ tbs. food coloring
  mixed to make
  brown/black

1. Spread the mixed seeds (except for the poppy seeds) evenly on a cookie sheet. Toast in a 400°F oven for 10 minutes. Allow to cool.

2. Put sugar and water in a saucepan over a low heat and stir until all the sugar has dissolved.

3. Turn the heat up and bring to a boil, without stirring. Be very careful, as boiling sugar is extremely hot. Stand back from the saucepan, but don't leave the kitchen, because the caramel always burns if you turn your back on it.

4. When it starts turning a beautiful golden color (about 10 minutes), add the lemon juice and food coloring. Add them quickly and then move your hand away immediately, as the mixture will spit and splutter like a live volcano. Have the adult help.

5. Quickly stir in the seeds (including the poppy seeds) and pour the mixture into a greased pan. Leave to cool and harden. When it is completely cold turn it out and break it into bite-size chunks. Keep it in an airtight container and it will remain delicious for days.

Pickled Spines of Porcupines

I'm mad for crispy wasp-stings on a piece of buttered toast,
*And **pickled spines of porcupines**. And then a gorgeous roast*
Of dragon's flesh, well hung, not fresh—it costs a pound at most,
(And comes to you in barrels if you order it by post).

—from JAMES AND THE GIANT PEACH

To avoid a crisis in this recipe, when you are painting the black bits on the porcupine spines do so very lightly, and with only a tiny amount of the food coloring. Otherwise, the spines get soggy and flop over like limp hair.

You will need:

electric beater

piping bag with a very
   small plain nozzle,
   or a small plastic bag

2 cookie sheets covered
   in nonstick baking
   parchment

small paintbrush or
   pastry brush

toothpick

4 egg whites

1 c. sugar

1¼ tsp. cornstarch

1¼ tsp. food coloring
   mixed to make
   brown or black

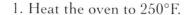

1. Heat the oven to 250°F.

2. Beat egg whites until stiff peaks form.

3. While beating, gradually add the sugar a little bit at a time. Beat until it's as stiff as the stiffest thing in the world, and then quickly beat in the cornstarch.

4. Fill piping bag with mixture and make 15 thin strips about 8″ long onto one of the cookie sheets. You won't use all of the mix—you still need to make the body, don't forget! If you don't have a piping bag just put the mixture into a small plastic bag and snip a tiny bit off the corner to squeeze out of. It doesn't matter if they are not perfectly straight, as these porcupine spines are pickled.

5. Make one big mound for the porcupine's body with the leftover mixture and place it on the other cookie sheet. Place both sheets in the oven.

6. Bake the spines for about 30 minutes, and then take them out and set them aside to cool. Leave the body in for a further 45 minutes or until the parchment peels away from the porcupine.

7. When the body is ready, take it out and allow to cool (approximately 10-15 minutes), then, using a toothpick, make tiny little holes for the spines.

8. Using the food coloring, paint 1″ long strips of black on the spines, leaving 1″ strips unpainted in between. Stick the spines into the little holes. The food coloring will soften the spines fairly quickly so this creation has a 10 minute viewing time before you have to eat it.

Doc Spencer's Pie

Not exactly like Doc Spencer's wife makes for him, but easier to eat if you're stuck somewhere in the wild with no knife and can't find Mrs. Doc Spencer.

MAKES 6

You will need:

pastry brush

baking sheet

4 slices of ham

4 hard boiled eggs

1¼ tbs. mayonnaise

2½ tsp. grated cheddar cheese

a dash of salt

1¼ tsp. freshly ground black pepper

phyllo dough (follow thawing instructions on package)

3 tbs. butter, melted

sesame seeds

1. Preheat oven to 400°F.

2. Chop ham and eggs into chunks.

3. Mix together ham, eggs, mayonnaise, cheddar cheese, salt, and pepper.

4. Cut 1 sheet of phyllo dough in half widthways. Lay one piece on top of the other.

5. Brush with melted butter. Put 2½ tbs. of egg and ham mix onto phyllo and carefully roll into a cigar shape, folding in the sides first so that it is safely sealed.

6. Brush the top with melted butter and sprinkle with sesame seeds. Continue until all the mixture is used up, or you lose interest. (The rest can be a sandwich filling.)

7. Bake in preheated oven for 15-20 minutes or until golden brown.

8. Allow to cool for 8 minutes before you eat it, otherwise you'll burn your tongue.

Very carefully, I now began to unwrap the greaseproof paper from around the doctor's present, and when I had finished, I saw before me the most enormous and beautiful pie in the world. It was covered all over, top, sides, and bottom, with a rich golden pastry.

—from DANNY THE CHAMPION OF THE WORLD

Pishlets

*They had a splendid effect upon the Pelican, for after he had
put one of them into his beak and chewed it for a while, he suddenly
started singing like a nightingale. This made him wildly excited
because Pelicans are not song-birds.*

—from THE GIRAFFE AND THE PELLY AND ME

You know that enormously annoying feeling you get when you know you want
to eat something, and you rack your brains but still can't decide what you want?
Next time this feeling strikes you down, don't stop to think, just run into the
kitchen without delay, put on an apron, and make up a batch of Pishlets.

You will need:

baking pan
saucepan

1½ sticks butter
⅔ c. brown sugar
1¼ tsp. baking soda
1 apple
1 pear
2¾ c. oats
½ c. raisins
½ c. dried cherries

1. Grease a baking pan with butter or shortening.

2. Preheat the oven to 350°F.

3. Melt the butter, sugar, and baking soda in a saucepan over low heat.

4. While the butter mixture is melting, peel the apple and pear and chop them into bite-size chunks.

5. Add the oats, raisins, dried cherries, apple, and pear to the saucepan and mix well.

6. Spoon into the baking pan and spread evenly.

7. Cook for about 25-30 minutes until golden on top.

8. Let it cool down and then cut into squares.

Plushnuggets

There were Gumtwizzlers and Fizzwinkles from China,
Frothblowers and Spitsizzlers from Africa, Tummyticklers and
Gobwangles from the Fiji Islands and Liplickers
*and **Plushnuggets** from the Land of the Midnight Sun.*

—from THE GIRAFFE AND THE PELLY AND ME

MAKES 12

You will need:

rolling pin

pastry brush

3″ circular cookie
  cutter

2 bananas

2½ tsp. maple syrup

2½ tsp. olive oil

1 package puff pastry
  (follow thawing
  instructions on
  package)

1 egg yolk

1. Squish the bananas with a fork and add maple syrup and olive oil.

2. Cut a 3″ circle out of the pastry with a cookie cutter.

3. On a floured surface, roll out the circle so it is 4″ across.

4. Put a blob of the banana mix in the middle of the dough. Lift up the edges of the circle and squash them together so they stick.

5. Use up the rest of the pastry in the same way.

6. Heat oven to 400°F. Put plushnuggets in the refrigerator until the oven is hot enough.

7. When oven is ready, brush plushnuggets with yolk and bake for about 20 minutes or until golden.

8. Allow them to cool for about 10 minutes before you eat them, as the middle remains very hot.

Strawberry Bonbons

The kind you can't find in any sweet shop.

*On the way to school and on the way back we always passed the sweet shop. No we didn't, we never passed it. We always stopped. We lingered outside its rather small window gazing in at the big glass jars full of Bull's-Eyes and Old Fashioned Humbugs and **Strawberry Bonbons** and Glacier Mints and Acid Drops and Pear Drops and Lemon Drops and all the rest of them.*

—from BOY

You will need:

food processor or
  blender

fine sieve

small saucepan

tray

nonstick baking
  parchment

toothpicks

1 adult

1½ c. whole
  strawberries, washed
  (you can use frozen
  whole strawberries,
  thawed)

1¼ c. sugar

9 tbs. water

⅓ tsp. liquid glucose, or
  corn syrup

1. Liquidize half of the strawberries and then push the purée through a very fine sieve, so that you don't have any of the seeds left.

2. Put the sugar, water, and liquid glucose into a small saucepan and stir over low heat until all the sugar is melted.

3. Turn the heat up and stop stirring.

4. While the sugar mixture is cooking, make sure that the remainder of the strawberries are completely dry. Place a sheet of nonstick baking parchment on a tray in preparation for the next stage.

5. When the sugar and water starts to turn golden (approximately 5 minutes), turn off the heat and stir in 2 tbs. of the puréed strawberry. Be very careful adding the purée, as it will spit, and it is extremely hot. Have the adult help.

6. Allow the mixture to cool for 10 minutes, and then put the whole strawberries onto toothpicks and dip into the sugar mixture. Place on the nonstick baking parchment to cool. These will start to ooze after about 15 minutes, so don't delay too long before eating!

Tummyticklers

There were Gumtwizzlers and Fizzwinkles from China,
*Frothblowers and Spitsizzlers from Africa, **Tummyticklers** and*
Gobwangles from the Fiji Islands and Liplickers and Plushnuggets
from the Land of the Midnight Sun.

—from THE GIRAFFE AND THE PELLY AND ME

This won't make you itchy like a toe tickle—it's a delicate delight to
soothe a hungry stomach. It's really like a toasted cheese stack, but
don't stop at cheese—you can put in any fillings you like, even sweet
ones, and you can have as many layers of tortillas in your
Tummyticklers as your mouth can fit around.
(This may require some training—nightly mouth stretching.)

24

You will need:

1 massive frying pan

3 soft flour tortillas
1 tbs. grainy mustard
1 tbs. mayonnaise
7½ tbs. grated cheddar
   cheese
2 finely sliced scallions
2 tsp. olive oil
freshly ground pepper

1. Spread mustard over one tortilla and mayonnaise over the other.

2. Sprinkle both with cheese.

3. Scatter the scallions over the tortilla with mayonnaise. Put one tortilla on top of the other, both with filling side up, and cover with the third tortilla.

4. Heat the massive frying pan, then add the oil.

5. Carefully transfer the stack of tortillas into the frying pan.

6. Cook over a medium heat until golden and crispy — about 2 minutes. Then turn it over and cook until golden brown on the other side. An easy way of turning it over is to place a plate big enough to cover the whole thing over the frying pan and then turn everything upside down, so that you end up with it on the plate. Then slide it back into the pan so the other side can cook. Be careful when doing this, as it is extremely hot.

7. Cut it into small slices like a cake and serve warm.

Boiled Slobbages

*I often eat **boiled slobbages**. They're grand when served beside*
Minced doodlebugs and curried slugs. And have you ever tried
Mosquitoes' toes and wampfish roes most delicately fried?
—from JAMES AND THE GIANT PEACH

A rare delicacy—by far the best slobbages in the land.

Note: The sauce needs to be prepared an hour ahead, and the slobbages can be prepared a few hours ahead and then reheated when you are ready to eat.

SERVES 3

You will need:

large saucepan

large bowl

colander

spatula

frying pan

slotted spoon

6 tomatoes

6 basil leaves

1 lb. ungrated
  mozzarella cheese

5 tbs. olive oil

salt and pepper

2 eggs

½ c. milk

¼ tsp. nutmeg

1½ c. flour

1. Chop tomatoes into small pieces.

2. Tear the basil leaves into small pieces.

3. Chop the mozzarella into small cubes.

4. Combine the tomato, mozzarella, basil, 3¾ tbs. of the olive oil, salt, and pepper.

5. Let this stand at room temperature for about an hour.

6. Meanwhile, mix together eggs, milk, salt, pepper, and freshly grated nutmeg.

7. Add the flour to the egg mixture. If it appears lumpy, use a whisk.

8. Let mixture rest in the refrigerator for 10 minutes.

9. Put a large saucepan of salted water on to boil.

10. Fill a large bowl with cold water.

11. When the water in the saucepan is boiling, hold the colander above the saucepan and pour the mixture into it, pushing it through into the boiling water with a spatula.

12. Simmer the slobbages for 2 minutes and then remove them with a slotted spoon and put them straight into the bowl of cold water for 15-30 seconds. Remove them with a slotted spoon and set the aside until you're ready to eat.

13. When you are ready to eat, drain the slobbages and heat them in a frying pan with the remaining olive oil.

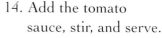

14. Add the tomato sauce, stir, and serve.

Glumptious Globgobblers

*To the Giraffe I gave a bag of **Glumptious Globgobblers**. The Globgobbler is an especially delicious sweet that is made somewhere near Mecca, and the moment you bite into it, all the perfumed juices of Arabia go squirting down your gullet one after the other.*

—from THE GIRAFFE AND THE PELLY AND ME

The traditional globgobbler is a delicious sweet. This variety, made in a secret location miles away from Mecca, is a mouth-watering savory treat.

You will need:

saucepan
food processor or blender
frying pan
paper towels
1 adult

1½ c. arborio rice
2 skinless and boneless
 chicken breasts
1¼ tbs. grated ginger or
 ½ tbs. dried ground ginger
1¼ tsp. medium curry powder
1 clove of garlic, crushed
3¾ tbs. roughly chopped
 coriander or 1½ tbs. dried
 coriander
4 scallions, sliced
5 tbs. corn
½ tsp. salt
freshly ground black pepper
½ c. light soy sauce
oil for deep-frying

1. Cook rice in 2½ c. of boiling salted water for 15 minutes and then rinse under cold running water until completely cold.

2. Place chicken breasts in food processor or blender and blend until smooth.

3. Add all other ingredients, except soy sauce and oil. Blend again for about 30 seconds.

4. Heat oil—about 1″ deep—in a deep frying pan. This would be the moment for an adult to help out.

5. While the adult is assisting you in the deep-frying department, rub a bit of cold oil on your hands and grab a walnut-size piece of the glumptious mix. Roll it into a ball. Continue until all the mixture is used up.

6. Stand back and hand over the globgobblers to the deep-frying department. The head of this department will then fry them until they are golden brown all over.

7. Drain on paper towels and sprinkle lightly with salt. Use soy sauce as a dip.

Toad-in-the-Hole

"By golly!" he cried. "That'll be the very first thing we'll make in our new oven! **Toad-in-the-hole!***"*

—from DANNY THE CHAMPION OF THE WORLD

I've never been lucky enough to see a toad in its hole, but I'm sure this is just how it looks.

MAKES 4

You will need:

frying pan

apple corer

tin foil

½ onion

½ leek

½ carrot

½ stick of celery

½ lb. ground beef or lamb

1¾ tsp. oil

1¼ tsp. tomato purée

1¼ tbs. Worcestershire sauce

salt

black pepper

4 baking potatoes, scrubbed clean

5 tbs. grated cheese

pat of butter

1. Heat the oven to 400°F.

2. Finely chop all the vegetables.

3. In a frying pan, brown the meat.

4. Remove the meat, and return any liquid to the pan. Add the oil and fry the vegetables until light brown.

5. Put the ground meat back into the pan with the vegetables. Add the tomato purée, Worcestershire sauce, a pinch of salt and a few turns of black pepper.

6. Allow to cool.

7. While the mixture is cooling, use the apple corer to make two long holes in each potato where the toad's eyes would be. Keep the bits you take out of the middle and trim them so that each one is 1″ long.

8. Push the meat into the holes in each potato and plug them up with the 1″ bits you have trimmed.

9. Wrap each potato in foil and bake for about 1¼ hours. Then unwrap the potatoes and place them back in the oven on top of the foil to crisp for a further 15 minutes. Take care when handling, as they will be extremely hot.

10. Cut each potato in half, cover in the grated cheese, the butter, and a bit more salt and pepper, and eat while hot.

Wonka's Whipple-Scrumptious Fudgemallow Delight

"Wonka's Whipple-Scrumptious Fudgemallow Delight!" cried
Grandpa George. "It's the best of them all! You'll just love it!"
—from CHARLIE AND THE CHOCOLATE FACTORY

The supreme queen of ice cream sauces!

You will need:

saucepan

long wooden spoon

large bowl of your
  favorite ice cream

2 squares dark
  chocolate

1 Heath Bar

½ stick butter

¼ c. dark brown sugar

⅔ c. heavy cream

8 marshmallows

1. Break the chocolate and the Heath Bar into large
   chunks and set to one side.

2. In a saucepan, over a low heat, melt together the
   butter, sugar, and cream.

3. Stir until all the sugar has dissolved and then turn
   the heat up and continue stirring for 10 minutes.
   Be careful, as the mixture gets very hot and can
   splutter. Use a very long wooden spoon or a tall
   adult with a long arm.

4. Turn the heat down again, and get your bowl of ice cream from the refrigerator.

5. Put the marshmallows, chocolate, and Heath Bar into the saucepan, stir around once and pour over your ice cream.

Note: You can keep any leftover sauce in the refrigerator and reheat it in the microwave.

Hot Noodles made from Poodles on a Slice of Garden Hose

For dinner on my birthday shall I tell you what I chose:
Hot noodles made from poodles on a slice of garden hose—
And a rather smelly jelly made of armadillo's toes.
(The jelly is delicious, but you have to hold your nose.)
—from JAMES AND THE GIANT PEACH

SERVES 2-3

You will need:

large saucepan
large bowl
slotted spoon
paper towels
food processor or
    blender
plastic wrap
rolling pin
2 coat hangers
colander

¼ c. flat leaf parsley
2 large eggs
1½ c. flour
1¼ tbs. olive oil
salt and pepper
1¼ tbs. Parmesan cheese

1. Bring a pan of water to a boil. Fill a large bowl with very cold water and have it ready next to the pan. When the water is boiling, drop the parsley into it—count to 5 and then take it out with a slotted spoon and drop straight into the bowl of very cold water.

2. Gather the parsley into a bunch and squeeze it very hard—you want to get all the water out—and then place it on a paper towel and set aside.

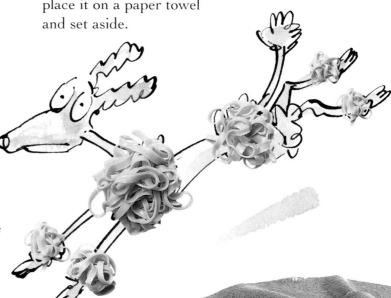

3. Put the eggs and flour into the food processor or blender and process for 2 minutes. You should have a soft but not sticky dough.

4. Take dough out of the machine and knead it on a lightly floured surface for a couple of minutes. Cover with plastic wrap and let it rest for 15 minutes.

5. After 15 minutes place about one quarter of the dough in the food processor or blender with the parsley, and whizz until the parsley is completely mixed into the dough, and the dough has turned garden-hose green. Take out and place on a floured surface. Using the rolling pin, roll it out as thinly as possible, and then cut into 2″ wide strips to make your flattened garden hose.

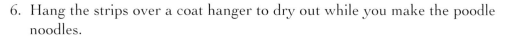

6. Hang the strips over a coat hanger to dry out while you make the poodle noodles.

7. Roll out the other batch of dough (the poodle) as thinly as possible and then roll up and slice into very thin rounds.

8. Unroll these rounds and hang on a coat hanger too. Allow to dry for 30 minutes.

9. Bring a very large saucepan of water to a boil and add 2 tsp. of salt, then put the garden hose in and cook at a rapid boil for 3-5 minutes.

10. Take out with a slotted spoon and drain in a colander.

11. Put the noodles in the boiling water and cook for 2-5 minutes depending on the thickness of the dough. Drain into the colander with the garden hose, and then put everything back into the saucepan, off the burner. Toss in the olive oil and some salt and pepper to taste.

12. Lay the garden hose onto a plate and top with the noodles and Parmesan.

Hot Dogs

I crave the tasty tentacles of octopi for tea
*I like **hot dogs**, I LOVE hot-frogs, and surely you'll agree*
A plate of soil with engine oil's a super recipe.
(I hardly need to mention that it's practically free.)
—from JAMES AND THE GIANT PEACH

No one can deny that hot dogs are one of the greatest things man has ever invented, *but* he made a mistake. No matter how hard you try, some of the ketchup or mustard always spills out in the end. This recipe is an essential for anyone who loves hot dogs but ends up with most of the filling on the carpet/in the dog's mouth/on the pavement/on the sparkling new trousers.

MAKES 8

You will need:

large bowl

roasting pan

rolling pin

pastry brush

1 packet of bread
dough mix

8 sausages

8 slices of bacon (only
if you like it in your
hot dog)

ketchup

mustard (your favorite
kind)

1 egg yolk

1. Preheat the oven to 400°F.

2. Follow instructions on side of bread mix for making
the dough.

3. While the dough is rising, put the sausages on the
roasting pan and put it in the oven. If you are using
the bacon, wrap it around the sausages before
cooking them. When they are light brown (about 15
minutes) take them out and allow to cool.

4. When the dough has doubled in size, divide it into
eight pieces, all the same size.

5. Roll each piece of dough into a 5-6″ wide circle.

6. Place one sausage in the middle of one circle of
dough and spread it with a small amount of ketchup
and/or mustard.

7. Carefully roll the dough around the sausage, keeping
it quite tight, and fold the sides in so that there is no
chance of escape.

8. Do the same with the rest of the sausages. Place in
the roasting pan.

9. Brush the dough with the egg yolk and allow to rise
again.

10. When the dough has doubled in size again (20-30
minutes), place in oven and cook for about 20-25
minutes or until golden.

11. Allow to cool for 5 minutes before eating—the
waiting is the only difficult part of the recipe. Set an
alarm clock and eat as soon as the bell goes off.

Grobswitchy Cake

"It is a little bit like mixing a cake," the BFG said. "If you is putting the right amounts of all the different things into it, you is making the cake come out any way you want, sugary, splongy, curranty, Christmassy or grobswitchy. It is the same with dreams."

—from THE BFG

SERVES 8

You will need:

mixing bowl

electric beater

8″ nonstick cake pan

5 tbs. soft brown sugar

1¼ tsp. ground
   cinnamon

2 sticks butter

¾ c. sugar

2 eggs

1¼ c. sour cream

1½ c. plain flour

½ c. self-raising flour

1¼ tsp. baking soda

1 c. chopped pecans

2½ tbs. grobswitchies
   (also known as amber
   sugar crystals)

1. Preheat oven to 325°F.

2. Mix together soft brown sugar and cinnamon and put to one side.

3. In a mixing bowl, cream butter and regular sugar together until pale and fluffy.

4. Add eggs one at a time to the butter mixture, mixing each time.

5. Stir in the sour cream. Sift the two kinds of flour and the baking soda in together.

6. Add half the mixture to the cake pan.

7. Sprinkle in half the cinnamon-and-sugar mix, half the chopped pecans, and half the grobswitchies.

8. Add the other half of the cake mix and then sprinkle the rest of the cinnamon and sugar, pecans, and grobswitchies on the top.

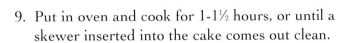

9. Put in oven and cook for 1-1½ hours, or until a skewer inserted into the cake comes out clean.

10. Allow to cool for about 15 minutes and then eat with some ice cream while still warm.

11. This cake keeps well for about a week.

Note: Grobswitchies remain hard even when cooked,
so be careful if you have false teeth!

A Plate of Soil with Engine Oil

I crave the tasty tentacles of octopi for tea
I like hot dogs, I LOVE hot-frogs, and surely you'll agree
A plate of soil with engine oil's *a super recipe.*
(I hardly need to mention that it's practically free.)
—from JAMES AND THE GIANT PEACH

SERVES 6

You will need:

loaf pan
mixing bowl
shallow pan
serving dish

1½ c. plain flour
1 c. soft brown sugar
½ c. cocoa powder
⅔ c. milk
3½ tbs. butter, melted
4 squares semi-sweet
  chocolate
1¾ c. hot milk
heavy cream

1. Grease the loaf pan.

2. Preheat the oven to 350°F.

3. Mix the flour and ¾ c. brown sugar with half the cocoa powder.

4. Beat in the cold milk and melted butter.

5. Break the chocolate into rough pieces and stir into the mixture.

6. Pour into the loaf pan.

7. Sprinkle ¼ c. brown sugar and the other half of the cocoa powder over the top of the mixture.

8. Pour the hot milk over it, place the loaf tin in a shallow roasting pan and bake for 1 hour 15 minutes. It is ready when the top feels crusty.

9. Carefully turn the whole thing out into a deep serving dish and eat it with cream while still hot.

Note: You can replace the dark chocolate with white chocolate if you prefer, or do a mixture of the two.

I find that old engine oil has a more refined taste than fresh.
When engine oil is fresh it is more like caramel which doesn't go
at all well with soil (not bad with fried ants though).

Luminous Lollies for Eating in Bed at Night

MAKES ABOUT 12

You will need:

food processor or blender

small plastic/disposable cups

plastic wrap

plastic forks

plastic spoons

nontoxic glow-in-the-dark paint (the type you can paint on plastic)

paintbrush

1 large ripe mango, chopped

⅓ c. dried mango, chopped

2½ tbs. powdered sugar

1¼ tsp. lemon juice

1. Put all the ingredients into the food processor or blender and whizz until smooth.

2. Fill the plastic cups to ½" below the top with the mango mix. Cover with plastic wrap and place in the freezer overnight.

3. Paint the prong end of the forks and the bowl end of the spoons to a third of the way up the handle. Allow to dry completely.

4. Take one of the plastic cups out of the freezer and cut down the side all around the edge at ½" intervals (you need to work quite quickly here so that you get to eat the lolly before it melts!). Tear down from the bits you have snipped so that the frozen mango lolly comes out easily.

5. Carefully place the frozen mango on a board and slice into 1" thick rounds.

6. Slip these over the non-painted bits of the spoons and forks, **making sure the food doesn't touch the paint**.

7. You can eat these straightaway or cover them and put them back in the freezer for another night.

Note: You should prepare these well in advance, as they need a whole night to freeze.

The Magic Green Crystal

Warning! These sacred treasures will be much in demand. Don't leave home without securing your lunchbox with an alarm and padlock. You can never be too careful when it comes to the magic green crystal.

You will need:

small saucepan
greased cookie sheet
knife

½ c. sugar
2½ tbs. corn syrup
1¼ tbs. lemon juice
3¾ tbs. water
½ tbs. green food
  coloring
1¼ tsp baking soda
oil

1. Put the sugar, syrup, lemon juice, and water into the saucepan. Stir over a low heat until all the sugar has dissolved.

2. Turn the heat up and boil without stirring until the mixture is a rich golden caramel brown (about 10 minutes).

3. Remove from the heat and quickly stir in the food coloring and then the baking soda—it will froth up right away.

4. Pour the mixture onto the cookie sheet and let it start to set.

5. Just before it hardens completely, cut it into diamonds with an oiled knife. Enjoy!

"Take a look, my dear," he said, opening the bag and tilting
it towards James. Inside it, James could see a mass of tiny green
things that looked like little stones or crystals.
—from JAMES AND THE GIANT PEACH

Nishnobblers

*There were **Nishnobblers** and Gumglotters and Blue Bubblers and Sherbet Slurpers and Tongue Rakers, and as well as all this, there was a whole lot of splendid stuff from the great Wonka factory itself.*
—from THE GIRAFFE AND THE PELLY AND ME

Nishnobblers are made from tempered chocolate. Tempering is when you mix melted and solid chocolate together to make it shinier and more manageable. It is an indispensable skill to have in life, and you learn how to do it right here! Once you've got the hang of it, you'll be able to create masterful chocolate constructions to rival Willy Wonka's.

MAKES 6

You will need:

microwave-safe bowl
or small saucepan

14"x11" sheet of
bubble wrap, cleaned
and dried

3" pastry cutter

pastry brush

4 oz. (4 squares) dark
chocolate

4 oz. (4 squares) white
chocolate

1. Melt 3 squares of the dark chocolate in a bowl on the defrost setting in the microwave, or over low heat in a small pan on the stove, stirring until melted. When it is melted, stir the unmelted block into it until the whole lot is smooth.

2. Paint over the bubble wrap sheet, using all the melted chocolate, and place it in the refrigerator for 15 minutes.

3. Melt the white chocolate in exactly the same way and then spread it over the dark chocolate. Chill this for 15 minutes.

4. Carefully peel the bubble wrap away from the chocolate and cut it into circles with the pastry cutter.

Butter Gumballs

*The sweet-shop of my dreams would be loaded from top to bottom with Sherbet Suckers and Caramel Fudge and Russian Toffee and Sugar Snorters and **Butter Gumballs** and thousands and thousands of other glorious things like that.*

—from THE GIRAFFE AND THE PELLY AND ME

These make great presents for parents, as they can't talk for ages while they chew and chew and chew. The recipe makes enough for you to keep a small supply for yourself as well.

You will need:

medium-size heavy
  bottomed saucepan

large tray

nonstick baking
  parchment or
  wax paper

tinfoil

plenty of time

1 can condensed milk
  (about 1 c.)

2½ tbs. brown sugar

2½ tbs. corn syrup

2 tbs. butter

1. Put all the ingredients into the saucepan and stir over a low heat until the mixture becomes a beautiful toffee color, and quite thick. This will take about 25-30 minutes. It is important that you stir for the whole time, otherwise it will burn at the bottom.

2. Cover a large tray with nonstick baking parchment. Put teaspoon-size blobs of the mixture onto the paper, spaced well apart.

3. Allow the blobs to get completely cold and then shape into balls by rolling them between your palms. If the mixture doesn't stay in shape it means that it needs to be cooked for a little longer, so put it back on the stove and start stirring all over again.

4. If you are going to give a few away as presents then cut squares of tinfoil and wrap each Butter Gumball up like a Christmas cracker.

Tongue Rakers

*There were Nishnobblers and Gumglotters and Blue Bubblers and Sherbet Slurpers and **Tongue Rakers**, and as well as all this, there was a whole lot of splendid stuff from the great Wonka factory itself.*

—from THE GIRAFFE AND THE PELLY AND ME

MAKES 1

You will need:

bowl, lightly greased

plastic wrap

small saucepan

sieve

rolling pin

large baking sheet

1 package of bread or pizza dough mix (whatever kind you like)

1 onion

2 cloves of garlic

1½ tbs. butter

1¼ tsp. salt

flour

1 egg yolk

1¼ tsp. rosemary

½ tsp. coarse salt

1. Heat the oven to 400°F.

2. Mix the bread dough according to the instructions on the packet. Knead for 8 minutes, and then place in a lightly greased bowl, cover with plastic wrap, and allow to rise until doubled in size (about 1 hour).

3. Meanwhile, finely chop the onion and garlic. Melt the butter in a small saucepan and add the onion and 1¼ tsp. salt. Cover, and cook over a very low heat for 15 minutes or until soft. Add the garlic and cook for 2 more minutes.

4. Drain the onion and garlic in a sieve over a bowl, and allow to cool.

5. When the dough has risen enough, add the cooled onion and garlic and knead again for 5 minutes. If the dough becomes sticky you may need to add a bit more flour—just enough to make it easy to knead.

6. Break off seven small pieces and one very large piece.

7. Roll the biggest piece so that it is the length of 1½ pencils, and a little bit thicker than a pencil.

8. Place this on the baking sheet.

9. Roll all the other pieces to the same thickness but half the length, and then attach these (by squishing) to one end of the long piece—just like you see in the picture. If your baking sheet is too small to do such a big one, you can just make it smaller. Tongue Rakers of all sizes are delicious.

10. Brush the Tongue Raker with the egg yolk, and sprinkle with rosemary and coarse salt.

11. Let the dough rise again, then bake until golden brown— about 20-25 minutes.

Note: You could use any leftover dough to make a loaf of bread. (This will probably take 30-35 minutes to cook.)

Lizards' Tails

I've eaten fresh mudburgers by the greatest cooks there are,
And scrambled dregs and stinkbugs' eggs and hornets stewed in tar,
*And pails of snails and **lizards' tails**, and beetles by the jar.*

—from JAMES AND THE GIANT PEACH

Roasted, grilled, curried, or stewed, the base of the tail and the toes are the best cuts.

MAKES 18

You will need:

food processor or blender
mixing bowl
baking sheet, lightly greased
pastry brush

1 lb. raw jumbo shrimp with
  the shell on (fresh or frozen)
1¼ tbs. fresh mint
1 clove of garlic
3 scallions
1 egg white
1¼ tsp. cornstarch
1¼ tsp. sugar
salt and pepper
oil

For the dip:

2½ tbs. fresh mint
½ mild chili pepper (de-seeded)
1¼ tbs. fish sauce
1¼ tsp. sugar
juice of 2 limes (3-4 tbs.)

1. Defrost shrimp completely (if using frozen ones).

2. Cut off the tail bit at the end of each shrimp and set aside in the refrigerator.

3. Peel the shrimp and place in the food processor or blender with the mint, garlic, scallions, egg white, cornstarch, sugar, and a pinch of salt and pepper. Process until smooth.

4. Cover and chill in the refrigerator for 20 minutes.

5. Prepare the dip: roughly chop the mint, finely chop the chili pepper. Mix together the mint, chili pepper, fish sauce, sugar, and lime juice. Cover and set aside.

6. Heat the broiler.

7. Wet your hands and shape the shrimp mix into tails (wetting your hands stops the mixture from sticking to you).

8. Place on a lightly greased baking sheet. Stick the shrimp tails into the mixture down the middle to make a long tail. Brush each lizard's tail with oil and place under the broiler for 5-7 minutes.

9. Eat with the dip.

Spitsizzlers

*There were Gumtwizzlers and Fizzwinkles from China, Frothblowers and **Spitsizzlers** from Africa, Tummyticklers and Gobwangles from the Fiji Islands and Liplickers and Plushnuggets from the Land of the Midnight Sun.*

—from THE GIRAFFE AND THE PELLY AND ME

Even better than chips!

You will need:

2 saucepans

colander

paper towels

large slotted spoon

1 adult to assist with
the deep-frying

7 oz. vermicelli

oil

2½ tsp. salt

2½ tsp. mild curry
powder

1. Cook the vermicelli in boiling salted water for 5 minutes. Drain into a colander and then run it under cold water to cool it down completely. Pour a teaspoon of oil over it and mix with your hands so that all the vermicelli is coated. This is to stop it from sticking together.

2. Lay it out on a paper towel and cover it with another layer of paper towel.

3. Have the adult pour oil into the second saucepan until it is about 3″ deep. Heat the oil so that it is hot enough for a small piece of vermicelli to sizzle and float to the top when you put it in.

4. Lay out more paper towels next to the saucepan you are going to use to deep-fry.

5. Mix together the salt and curry powder.

6. Have the adult add a tangle of vermicelli to the oil. As soon as it hits the oil it will sizzle and spit and rise to the top. Carefully turn it over with the slotted spoon, leave for 1-2 minutes, and then take out and place on the paper towel (it should not be brown, just stiff). Sprinkle with a large pinch of the salt and curry powder mix. Continue until all the vermicelli is used up.

Sherbet Slurpers

*There were Nishnobblers and Gumglotters and Blue Bubblers and **Sherbet***
***Slurpers** and Tongue Rakers, and as well as all this, there was a whole lot*
of splendid stuff from the great Wonka factory itself.

—from THE GIRAFFE AND THE PELLY AND ME

You might want to put your laboratory coat on for this recipe—it's
more of a chemistry process than a cooking one! Once the mixture
is made it is scooped into straws, which are then sealed—the
perfect size to stash in a pocket for an emergency slurp.

MAKES 5

You will need:

5 plastic straws

1 cigarette lighter or a
   book of matches

1 adult

½ tsp. citric acid
   (available from
   pharmacies) or you
   can use lemon zest

4 Sweetarts, crushed to
   a fine powder

¼ tsp. baking soda

1-2 tsp. powdered sugar

1. Ask an adult to seal one end of all the straws by
   melting it and then pressing it together with his/her
   fingers. The plastic does get hot, so the flame should
   be held to it for just a couple of seconds before the
   edges are pressed together.

2. Mix together the first 3 ingredients and then add 1 tsp. of powdered sugar. Taste the mixture before you add more, as this may already be sweet enough for you. Don't add too much sugar, or the fizz will disappear.

3. Fold a large piece of paper and then pour the Slurper mix into the fold. Get it into the straw by scooping the straw along through the mix and tapping the closed end on the counter top between each scoop.

4. As each one is filled, ask the adult to seal the other end in the same way as before.

5. When you are ready to slurp your sherbet, open up one end of the straw and insert into mouth.

Bean's Cider

*"You're poaching," shrieked Rat.
"Put that down at once! There'll be none left for
me!" Rat was perched upon the highest shelf in
the cellar, peering out from behind a huge jar.
There was a small rubber tube inserted in
the neck of the jar, and Rat was using this
tube to suck out the cider.*

—from FANTASTIC MR. FOX

MAKES 1 MUG

You will need:

small saucepan

fine mesh sieve

peeler

food processor or
blender

strong arms

4 apples—a sweet
variety

juice of 1 lime (2 tbs.)

2½ tbs. light brown
sugar

1 cinnamon stick
broken into 3 pieces

apple juice

1. Peel and core the apples.

2. Place in food processor or blender with lime juice
and puree for 4 minutes.

3. Push through a very fine sieve into a
small saucepan.

4. Add 2½ tbs. of brown sugar and the broken
cinnamon stick.

5. Heat gently on low while stirring.

6. Push through a sieve again—if it is too thick to
drink, add some apple juice and stir.

7. Pour into a mug—and it's ready.

Devil's Drenchers

*When you have sucked a **Devil's Drencher** for a minute or so, you can set your breath alight and blow a huge column of fire twenty feet into the air.*

—from THE GIRAFFE AND THE PELLY AND ME

The great thing about a Devil's Drencher is that it is two recipes in one. When you first make it you eat it with a spoon, and if it melts before you finish it, it magically transforms into a delicious drink which you can suck through a straw. Wouldn't it be incredible if that happened with other recipes—like a roast chicken changing into a chocolate mousse when you get down to the last wing?

MAKES 1½ PINTS

You will need:

1 long wooden skewer
blender or food
  processor
drinking glass

6 licorice laces
9 strawberry laces
2 c. frozen raspberries
  (you can freeze the
  berries yourself or
  buy them frozen)
2 c. frozen cranberries
juice of 3 oranges
½ c. powdered sugar

1. Twist all the licorice laces and 6 of the strawberry laces into a rope, and tightly wrap it around the length of the wooden skewer. Pinch them together at the top.

2. Cut the 3 remaining strawberry laces in half and drape over the top of the skewer. You will need to balance this in a glass while you make the quenching Drencher.

3. Place all remaining ingredients in the food processor or blender and process until smooth.

4. Quickly spoon into the glass with the laced skewer.

5. Eat or drink.

Note: This mixture can be pushed through a fine sieve if you don't like the seeds.

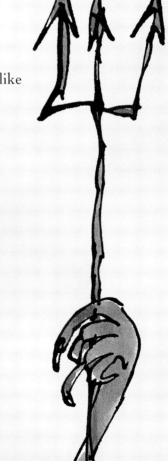

Liquid Chocolate Mixed by Waterfall

Charlie put the mug to his lips, and as the rich warm creamy chocolate ran down his throat into his empty tummy, his whole body from head to toe began to tingle with pleasure, and a feeling of intense happiness spread over him.

—from CHARLIE AND THE CHOCOLATE FACTORY

SERVES 1

You will need:

rolling pin
saucepan
whisk

4 oz. milk chocolate
½ c. milk
1 Kit Kat

1. While the milk chocolate is still in its packaging, batter it with a rolling pin. If using part of a larger package, put it in a sealed plastic baggy, then hit it.

2. Put the chocolate bits into a saucepan and add the milk. Stir over a low heat until all the chocolate is melted.

3. Whisk the mixture to make it frothy and then pour it into the biggest mug you can find.

4. Use the Kit Kat as a stirrer.

Fizzy Lifting Drinks

"Oh, those are fabulous!" cried Mr. Wonka. "They fill you with bubbles, and the bubbles are full of a special kind of gas, and this gas is so terrifically lifting that it lifts you right off the ground just like a balloon, and up you go until your head hits the ceiling—and there you stay."

"But how do you come down again?" asked little Charlie.

"You do a burp, of course," said Mr. Wonka.

—from CHARLIE AND THE CHOCOLATE FACTORY

SERVES 1

You will need:

cream soda
vanilla ice cream

1. Close all the doors so that you don't end up on the moon.

2. Fill a glass ¾ full with cream soda.

3. Top with a giant scoop of vanilla ice cream.

4. Drink.

5. Burp.

Blue Bubblers

There were Nishnobblers and Gumglotters and
Blue Bubblers *and Sherbet Slurpers.*

—from THE GIRAFFE AND THE PELLY AND ME

SERVES 1-2

You will need:

1 large glass
1 long wooden skewer

juice of 2 lemons
1 liter of seltzer
    water (4 c.)
sugar to taste
blue food coloring
10 blueberries
10 blackberries

1. Squeeze lemons.
   Add the juice to the
   seltzer water and
   add sugar until it's
   sweet enough for you.

2. Add enough food
   coloring so that it is the
   perfect shade of blue
   (you won't need a lot).

3. Carefully thread the berries onto the skewer, alternating between the
   blueberries and the blackberries. The length of skewer you can use will
   depend on the height of your glass.

4. Place the skewer into the glass and let cocktail hour officially begin. . . .